OLYMPIA SOUTH
103 NE FIFTH ST.
ATLANTA, IL 61723-9712
(217) 648-2302
(217) 648-5248 (FAX)

THE VALUE OF LOVE

The Story of Johnny Appleseed

VALUE COMMUNICATIONS, INC.
PUBLISHERS
LA JOLLA, CALIFORNIA

THE VALUE OF LOVE

The Story of
Johnny Appleseed

BY ANN DONEGAN JOHNSON

THE DANBURY PRESS

The Value of Love is part of the ValueTales series.

The Value of Love text copyright © 1979 by Ann Donegan Johnson. Illustrations copyright © 1979 by Value Communications, Inc.

First Edition
Manufactured in the United States of America
For information write to: ValueTales, P.O. Box 1012
La Jolla, CA 92038

Library of Congress Cataloging in Publication Data

Johnson, Ann Donegan.
    The value of love.

    (ValueTales series)
    SUMMARY: A biography of John Chapman whose distribution of appleseeds and trees across the Midwest made him a legend and left us a legacy we can still enjoy today.
        1.   Chapman, John, 1774-1845—Juvenile literature.
2.   Apple growers—United States—Biography—Juvenile literature.   3.   Frontier and pioneer life—Middle West —Juvenile literature.   [1.   Chapman, John, 1774-1845.
2.   Apple growers.   3.   Frontier and pioneer life.
4.   Love]   I.   Title.
SB63.C46J63   635'.092'4   [92]   [B]   78-31873

ISBN 0-916392-35-X

4

To John Carey
who really would have understood
Johnny Appleseed.

This tale is about a very loving person, Johnny Appleseed. The story that follows is based on events in his life. More historical facts about Johnny Appleseed can be found on page 63.

Once upon a time...

so long ago that most of our country was still a wilderness, a little boy was busy growing up in a tiny, crowded cabin in a small but bustling community in Massachusetts.

The boy's name was John Chapman, and of course everyone called him Johnny. And even when he was very young, he wasn't quite like other boys.

"He's given to wondering and dreaming," said the neighbors. "What a restless child! Like as not Mistress Chapman will have her troubles with that lad!"

7

But Johnny's stepmother paid no attention to the gossips. "Johnny's a loving boy," she said to herself as she watched him with his little brothers and sisters. "There's no one better to rock a cradle or sing a lullaby."

Johnny was a willing boy, too. He was always ready to run to the wood pile and bring back logs for the fire, or to scamper to the well when his stepmother needed a pail of water.

True, the boy was a dreamer, so he had his troubles with the schoolmaster. But on the whole he got along well enough, and before he was very old he had learned to do his sums and to read his Bible. And it turned out that reading the Bible was a thing Johnny dearly loved to do.

When he wasn't in school, or at his chores, or helping with the newest baby in the family, Johnny liked to go off into the woods by himself. He would sit under a tree and read the Bible out loud.

Strangely enough, the animals sometimes came to listen. Then Johnny would leave off reading and he would start to tell them what it was like in heaven, and how surely even the squirrels and the badgers must have a place there. For didn't the Lord make them all?

The birds sat on the low branches just above Johnny's head and they listened. The rabbits crept close to Johnny's feet. Sometimes a young deer stalked out of the forest and stood staring at the dark-haired boy with the big book.

One especially fine autumn afternoon, when the sun was warm in the clearings, a jay flew down and perched on Johnny's shoulder. It made a noisy, chattering, scolding sound, as jays often do. Then it flew up and away and was gone.

A raccoon was washing a crayfish in the stream nearby. He looked around as the jay flew off. "I think," said the raccoon, "that bird was trying to tell you something."

"I guess he was telling me goodbye," said Johnny softly. "It's time for him to fly south before the snows come."

Then Johnny suddenly realized that he was sitting there having a chat with a raccoon. While it's true that Johnny often talked to the animals, he was more than a bit startled to hear one talk back to him—and in his own language!

"My name is Randy," said the raccoon, "and I've been watching you for quite a while. I'd like to be your friend. I don't suppose you'd mind having a furry friend, would you?"

13

Now deep down in his heart Johnny knew that raccoons talk
in raccoon talk, and not in plain, ordinary English. He knew
he had made Randy up. But he needed a friend who would
understand how it was with him—how he liked to wander by
himself and dream big dreams of exploring the land that lay to
the west of Massachusetts. It was wild land, where the forests
grew so thick that someone who walked under the trees might
think it was twilight all the day long.

So when Johnny set out for home, he took Randy with him.
And when he came in sight of the cabin where he lived, it was
swarming with youngsters, and there was a wagon out in front.

"It's Pa!" cried Johnny. "He's come home from his trip!"

Johnny began to run, for he loved his father very much. Next to the times when he was in the woods, he liked the times he was in his father's carpentry shop, watching Nathaniel Chapman make bowls and churns and spice boxes for the good folks in the settlements up and down the state.

"When you get a mite bigger," his father always told him, "you can come with me to help sell my woodenware."

15

Johnny wasn't quite big enough yet, so that day he just helped his father unhitch the old horse from the wagon and lead it into the barn. "Maybe when I go in the springtime," said Johnny's father, "you can come with me."

Then Mr. Chapman went into the house.

Randy the raccoon watched while Johnny rubbed the horse down with handfuls of straw. "You're a good old boy," said Johnny, and he kissed the horse on the nose. "Next spring," he said. "Next spring I can go with Pa!"

16

Johnny held the thought all during that autumn, while the apples ripened on the trees. He helped with the picking that year, and he saw his stepmother string some of the apples up in the kitchen to dry, so there would be applesauce during the winter. Some of the apples went into the cellar, where they would keep better. They would be baked into pies. And the apples that fell to the ground were taken to a mill, where the pulp was pressed and the juice ran out to make apple cider.

"Was anything ever as good as apples?" said Johnny. "I think the Lord must have put them on earth to give us joy!"

"Of course he did," said Randy the raccoon, and since Johnny always told him that the Lord loved everybody the same, Randy helped himself to a nice, red apple from Johnny's basket.

When winter came, the spinning wheel in the Chapman cabin hummed and the weaver's loom thumped. Johnny's stepmother was making cloth.

"New clothes for you, Johnny," she said. "You can't go about in rags like a scarecrow."

Johnny loved his stepmother and he was grateful for the new clothes she made for him. He tried to keep himself tidy, and to remember to comb his hair.

But Johnny's mind was never really on how he looked. At night, when Johnny and Randy climbed to their bed in the loft over the cabin, Johnny whispered his dreams to Randy. "The trip with Pa will be just the beginning," he said. "Someday I'm going to travel west, way out to Ohio, where the land is still new. When I'm old enough to carry a gun, then I can go."

"Old enough to carry a gun?" cried Randy. "Can this be the John Chapman who reads the Bible to his forest friends? The one who claims that the Lord loves everybody the same? Don't you think your fellow creatures have just as much right to live as you do?"

19

Johnny thought about these words all during the long winter, and he decided Randy was right. "I'll never carry a gun," he resolved. "I'll never shoot a living thing."

Spring came, and it was time for Johnny to set out with his father to sell the woodenware. Johnny was thrilled. He had never before been away from his home. Of course Randy was with him, and so he and Johnny both saw the family of pioneers on the road near Springfield.

The pioneers had a great Conestoga wagon and a team of oxen. They had piles and piles of household goods and supplies aboard the wagon. But they weren't going anywhere when Johnny and Randy saw them. They were simply standing in the meadow beside the road, looking up at the pink blossoms on the apple trees.

"They look so sad," said Johnny to Randy. "Don't they know that going west will be a great adventure?"

"They know," said Randy. "They just have to say goodbye to the things they're leaving behind—like apple trees."

"No apple trees in the wilderness?" asked Johnny.

"No apple trees in the wilderness," said Randy. "Only forest trees like beech and oak and fir. And those trees have to crowd each other just to get room to grow!"

Johnny thought about this and his heart was heavy. No apple trees blooming in the springtime. No fruit growing through the warm summer. No fresh apples to eat in the fall. No cider. No apple butter or applesauce in the long, hard winter.

Johnny felt a great surge of love and pity for that pioneer family. "No apples," said he, in a small, sad voice as he watched them set out in their wagon.

"You have to give up something if you want to make your way in a new land," said Randy.

"Someday I'll do something about that!" declared Johnny. "I'll see that no one has to give up apples!"

In the years that followed, Johnny often went with his father and helped sell the woodenware. And Randy went along and watched Johnny grow. And when he was a strapping lad in his teens, Johnny set out to work on his own.

Can you guess what he did?

He hired himself out to a man who knew everything there was to know about orchards. And when Johnny worked for that man, he didn't do any daydreaming. He paid attention!

Soon he knew how deep to plant apple seeds. He knew how much to water the warm earth so that the seeds would sprout. He learned how to tend the orchards once they started, and to set the young trees far enough apart from one another. He learned to prune the trees, and he learned that if he wanted to move a tree he would have to wrap the roots well in wet moss so that they wouldn't dry out.

When he was eighteen, Johnny felt that he was ready. "Nathaniel," he said to his younger brother, "come springtime I'm setting out for Olean. That's way off in the western part of New York State. Pa's brother Ben lives there. Want to come along?"

Now there was no very good reason for Johnny to take Nathaniel along. The boy was only eleven. "Can't think why I'm doing it," said Johnny to Randy.

"Because the boy's fond of you and he wants to go," said Randy. "You love him too, or I'm much mistaken."

Johnny did love his brother, so when April came, he and Nathaniel said goodbye to their folks. Mr. Chapman read a special verse out of the Bible, and he asked the Lord to look after his two boys.

Johnny felt a twinge of loneliness, for it was no small thing to leave the people he held dear.

"You'll be fine!" said his father. "You're a good lad and you're bound to do well. Now if the farmland in the west is as rich as people say, send word and we'll come!"

Johnny promised that he would, and he and Nathaniel set out, with Randy scampering along behind.

The boys went on foot, and everywhere he looked Johnny saw the forest trees growing tall, shutting out the sky. "It would be welcome to see an

apple tree instead," he said. "There should be clearings and orchards in them."

"I have a feeling that there will be clearings," said Randy. He didn't particularly object to forest trees—although he liked orchards as well as anyone.

After a long, long journey, Johnny and Nathaniel and Randy reached Olean, and they had a surprise.

What do you think it was?

The cabin where Ben Chapman had settled years before was empty.

"What a disappointment!" said Randy. "I'll bet your uncle's gone to the new land around the Ohio River. Why don't you rest for a bit and then go after him?"

What Randy said made good sense to Johnny—perhaps because when he listened to Randy he was really listening to his own good sense. "We'll need supplies," he said, "so we'll have to get work. But we can do it."

Johnny surely could do it. He knew so much about planting and pruning that a farmer in Olean was glad to hire him. That fall, when the apple crop was harvested, Johnny drove a wagon loaded with apples to the cider mill. When the apples were ground to pulp and the cider was pressed out, Johnny saw that there were apple seeds everywhere around the mill.

"Each one is really an apple tree, just waiting to find its place in the earth so it can grow," he told Randy. "It's a shame to let seeds go to waste."

Johnny gathered up every seed that he could. He washed the seeds and dried them and put them in a sack. And from that day on, Johnny never threw away an apple seed.

The next spring, Johnny and Nathaniel and Randy set out on their travels again. Their uncle had talked of farming the land near Marietta, in Ohio. The boys had decided to look for him there.

Sometimes they traveled with pioneer families. Then Johnny helped drive the great wagons. Sometimes they walked. Sometimes they went by water, for the rivers were like highways in the unsettled land.

30

To use the river roads the boys needed a canoe, and Johnny was skilled at making dugouts. He and Nathaniel first chopped a hole in a fallen log. Then they built a fire in the hole to hollow the log out so that it would float upright.

"Say what you like," said Randy, "but pioneering isn't a life for lazy folks."

"Lazy folks can sit at home and let moss grow on them," laughed Johnny. "Nat and I, we aim to see the green land that's out west. And if it's a fine country for farming, I'll send word to Pa, just as I promised."

31

Johnny and Nathaniel would be off in their dugout then, with Randy riding in the prow, watching the river for whirlpools or shallows that might upset them. Time and again as they went along, Johnny talked about how grand the forests would look when they had clearings in them, and homesteads, and apple trees growing in the clearings.

"An apple orchard that's planted properly and pruned with love—why, it will live and bless people for most of a hundred years," he told Randy.

Johnny and Nathaniel came to Marietta at last, and they found Ben Chapman in the town on a market day. Uncle Ben was so delighted to see his brother's boys, and to hear that his brother might come, too, and settle in the rich land along the Ohio, that he danced a jig right there in the street.

"My goodness!" said Randy. "That's a whooping and a welcoming the likes of which I've never seen. That man's right glad to see kinfolk way out here on the frontier!"

The boys sent word to their father that the land near Marietta was very fine. Back in Massachusetts, Nathaniel Chapman made plans for the long trek west with his family. He would settle on Duck Creek near Marietta, and he would be happy there.

But for Johnny there would be no settling. He was as restless as when he'd tramped the woods as a boy. "It's time I began my life's work," he said to Randy.

"You'll need tools," said Randy, who knew quite well what Johnny's life's work would be. "A shovel, an ax, and a hoe."

Johnny nodded. "And I'll need my Bible."

"You plan to preach to the animals some more?" asked Randy.

"Why not?" said Johnny. "That's how I met you. But I'll find people to read the Bible with me. Wait and see!"

So Johnny tucked his good book into his shirt. By now he had a sack bursting with apple seeds, and he slung this onto his shoulder, together with a sack filled with corn meal. He picked up his tools, and since he had no other place to put his cooking pot, he wore it on his head—and a very fine hat it was.

And Johnny at last began his real wandering.

For a while he worked in western Pennsylvania. He had his nurseries there, with thousands of tender young trees. And he would always come back there, never passing a cider mill without searching through the pulp for seeds.

But it was the unbroken wilderness that really drew Johnny. He thought of the pioneers who would come after him. He thought how delighted they would be to see apple trees. He thought of the children, and how they could climb the trees in the autumn and crunch the ripe apples in their teeth.

Johnny's clothes wore out and his shoes went to pieces, and he didn't care. He tramped through Ohio, preparing the earth, planting seeds, watering his orchards and tending them. When he finished, he moved on to do it again in some new place.

He was a loving friend to his little trees, however. He always came back to them. When they were two years old they had to be replanted so that there was enough distance between them. Johnny always saw to this. Then he pruned them and fussed over them like a kind father fussing over his beloved children.

Sometimes Johnny gave his trees away. If a man was poor, and if he had children to feed and a wife whose life needed some joy in it, there would be trees from Johnny. The children could play under the boughs in the summer. They could run to gather the windfalls when they began to come down with the autumn winds.

Sometimes Johnny sold his trees. He needed to eat, just like anyone else. If a settler had money and could pay, Johnny got a good price for his trees.

And what did he do with the money?

Well of course a bit of it went for corn meal, for Johnny Chapman was mighty fond of corn pone. Indeed, he almost lived on it—that and apples.

But corn meal doesn't cost that much. Johnny did something else with his money. Can you guess what it was?

He bought animals with it—horses and mules and oxen that couldn't pull heavy burdens along the rough trails any more. Johnny loved them, just the way he loved children and apple trees. If he heard of a horse being abused or abandoned, he bought it—then gave it to some farmer who would be kind to it.

That's what Johnny did with his money.

Sometimes Johnny would plant an orchard on the land of a man who needed trees. "Now half of these trees are yours," he would tell the delighted settler, "but half of them are mine, and I may be sending for them."

Johnny would wait then until he met a farmer with half a dozen children hungering for the taste of an apple, and a wife who hadn't seen apple blossoms since she was a bride. Johnny would give the farmer a slip of paper. "It's an order for some trees," he would say. "You take it to Jabez Higgins down on the turnpike, and he'll let you have twenty young saplings."

That's the way Johnny sent for his trees.

41

Soon Johnny was known all through the frontier. It seemed that no matter how far west the settlers pushed, he had been there before them. And strange tales were told about him.

They said that the wolves came snuffling around his campfire at night when he sat eating his corn pone, and they never harmed him. They said he called himself brother to the bear, and that he could understand the crows when they chattered to one another about the doings of the forest creatures.

Whether the tales were true or not, no one ever knew for sure.
Johnny didn't talk much of his own affairs. But one thing is
certain: When he came striding out of the woods with his
cooking pot on his head and his sack of appleseeds on his
back, the children all ran out to greet him.

"Johnny Appleseed!" they cried. "Here he comes! Johnny
Appleseed! Hello, Johnny!"

The settlers always made a great fuss about Johnny. He was welcome in every cabin, and he had the best place by the fire. The children gathered close as he ate his corn pone and apple fritters and wild honey. When he had eaten, he read verses from the Bible. And then he told the news.

They were starved for news on the frontier—for talk of the important things that were happening far away in the east, in Washington, where the great men of government lived.

Not that Johnny ever got to Washington, or anywhere near it. He didn't. But he met people on the trails and the turnpikes who did, and he passed their news along to the settlers.

When the serious question of news was taken care of, Johnny might spin a few yarns of his own. The children always laughed when he told about the boy who caught a fish so big that he had to carry it over his shoulder while its tail dragged on the ground. "He had a fish fry that lasted three days, and when it was done he sold the bones to a keelboat skipper to use for an oar!"

Johnny Appleseed knew the Indians as well as he knew the white settlers. From them he learned the art of making medicines to soothe burns and of brewing herb teas to cure sickness. And the Indians respected him, for he was a peaceful man.

Just because he was peaceful, Johnny was troubled when bad feelings arose between the Indians and the white settlers. The Indians resented it when the white people took over their land. As Johnny went his way with his tools and his apple seeds, he saw that the Indians were preparing for war. He heard them speak of the white men with hatred.

"There will be fighting," said Randy one evening, as he sat with Johnny beside a campfire. "The birds talk about it in the trees, and the squirrels tell of seeing a war party in the north. Johnny Appleseed, what will you do if there is war between your red brothers and your white ones?"

It was a hard question. It made Johnny's heart heavy. "I will do whatever I can to stop it," he decided, "but I will not lift a hand against anyone, red or white!"

Soon after, Johnny saw Indians wearing their war paint. Their faces were stern and angry.

"It's happening!" whispered Randy. "They're going to attack the settlers' cabins!"

"The stockade at Mansfield isn't far away," said Johnny. "I'll warn the settlers. They can go to the stockade, which the Indians won't be so quick to attack."

Johnny began to run, and for once in his life he didn't worry about apple seeds. If some spilled out of his sack, he never noticed. He raced from cabin to cabin. "The Indians are getting ready to attack!" he cried. "Hurry! Drop everything! Run to the stockade!"

The settlers raced to the stockade, and when the Indians came swooping down on the cabins they found emptiness. There was no one to fight them. There was no killing. The settlers were safe for the moment.

But they wouldn't be safe for long.

"There aren't enough of us to stand off an attack if the Indians bring more warriors," said one man inside the stockade. "Besides, we can't stay here forever. We're short of food and water. Someone has to go to the fort at Mount Vernon and bring back the soldiers."

But Mount Vernon was a small settlement thirty miles away. The settlers thought of the journey through dense woods and across half-cleared land, and their hearts went cold.

Then Johnny Appleseed spoke up. He had been standing quietly near the gate with his cooking pot on his head. "I'll go," he said. "If it will save a single life, I'll go."

He set out right away. He traveled all day and all night. He never seemed to hurry, yet he covered the ground quickly. The Indians saw him and they let him pass unharmed. He was a peaceful man, and they could not think of him as their enemy.

The soldiers at Mount Vernon were terribly excited when they heard of the settlers in trouble at Mansfield. They ran to get their weapons and to check their ammunition.

"But we'll need someone to guide us," said one officer to Johnny. "Can you show us the way to Mansfield?"

Johnny groaned a weary groan.

"You can do it," whispered his little friend Randy. "Rest for a while and then you'll feel strong again."

Johnny nodded. "Give me an hour, and some food and water," he told the officer. "Then I'll be ready to set out."

After an hour Johnny *was* ready. And again he walked for a day and a night through the forest.

When the soldiers arrived at Mansfield, the Indian attack had already begun. The men from Mount Vernon charged into the fight with blazing guns, and the Indians fled. But when the smoke cleared, Johnny Appleseed was gone, too. He had done all he could to keep the peace. But when fighting broke out anyway, he vanished into the woods.

Fortunately, the hard times on the frontier did not last forever. Peace came again, and once more Johnny was seen in the settlements with his apple seeds. Again he tended his trees and stopped at the farms to visit with the children.

And so the years went by. Johnny's black hair turned gray, and the children he dandled on his knee when he visited the homesteads in Ohio and Indiana and Illinois—why, they were the children and the grandchildren of youngsters he'd met on the trails when he was a young man himself.

"We're getting old, do you know that, Johnny Appleseed?" said his friend Randy.

"A man's bound to if he lives long enough," declared Johnny.

One spring day, Johnny was tending his trees in the land near
Fort Wayne, in Indiana. There had been a late snow that year,
wet and heavy, and it took all of Johnny's love and faith to
remember that soon the land would be filled with the pink
sweetness of apple blossoms.

"Strange," said Johnny. "I feel a kind of weariness in my heart. I think I'll sit down for a spell and rest."

Then he and Randy sat together under one of the trees.

A farmer found Johnny there. He was hot with a fever. The man took him home to a simple shack he sometimes used when he was in the neighborhood. He gave Johnny herb teas and some of the other remedies that Johnny had once given him. But it wasn't any use.

"Johnny Appleseed died last night," said the farmer to his neighbors the next day. "He went just as peacefully as he lived!"

"Maybe he thinks there are apple trees in heaven," said one of the neighbors.

"And who's to say there aren't?" asked his wife.

The word was passed from village to village. Johnny Appleseed had died quietly—as quietly as he did everything else. He was taken sick while sitting under one of his own trees. He was seventy-one years old.

That might be the end of Johnny's story, except that people just plain couldn't forget him. Not good, gentle Johnny, with his sack of apple seeds and his wonderful stories. Not Johnny with his kind hands on the brow of a sick child. Not Johnny who loved red people and white so much he wouldn't fight either of them—though he'd walk thirty miles through the wilderness and thirty miles back again to save both from harm.

And so Johnny Appleseed became a legend.

Johnny had walked with love all his life—the love he felt for
every creature that lived on earth. That love lasted even after
he was gone.

Today there are schools named after Johnny Appleseed. Parks
and gardens and orchards have been laid out and planted in
his honor. No doubt they would please Johnny.

And surely it would please him to sit in one of the orchards and watch the sun come golden through the leaves. No doubt he would like to have a child or two close to him to listen to his tales. It was the trees growing and the children gathered near him that made him happiest all his life long.

The frontier days are over now, and unless you plan to plant apple trees on the moon, you can't do exactly what Johnny did. But you can think about your own life and about the people you love. You may want to find a way to show that love, and perhaps to be more loving to more people. If you do, chances are that your love will be returned. And when you give love and receive it, you may find that you're a happier person.

Just like our good friend Johnny Appleseed.

The End

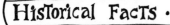

America is a land of legends, and legends have a way of being larger than life. Paul Bunyan was sixty-three ax handles high, and when he dragged his pick across the earth in Arizona we got the Grand Canyon. Pecos Bill came roaring out of Texas, lassoed a tornado and tamed it down to a breeze.

But then there's Johnny Appleseed, and he is a folk hero of quite a different sort. He was never a brawler or a doer of mighty deeds. And he is not a myth. Unlike Paul Bunyan and Pecos Bill, Johnny really existed.

He was born John Chapman in Massachusetts in 1774. He was an obscure lad from an obscure family, so much of his early life is undocumented. His father is supposed to have fought with General Washington during the American Revolution, and his mother died when Johnny was still a toddler. His father soon remarried, so Johnny and his older sister Elizabeth grew up in a household which included many younger half-brothers and half-sisters.

Tradition has it that Johnny was a solitary child, and that he liked to wander away from home and take long trips into the woods, where he studied the habits of the birds and the animals.

The journey which Johnny and his brother took to Olean when Johnny was eighteen was a marvelous adventure for the boys. They crossed New York State on foot, probably walking west from Albany.

Johnny's whereabouts in the years immediately after the Olean journey are uncertain, but when he was about twenty-five he appeared in the Ohio River valley and began his life's work—reading the Bible to settlers in the new land, and planting apple trees all through the frontier.

Johnny was to continue his planting and his preaching for almost fifty years. He was a familiar figure to the pioneers, and the Indians respected him and looked upon him as a medicine man, for he planted herbs at the same time that he planted apple trees, and he could brew soothing teas and make poultices to heal wounds and burns.

JOHNNY APPLESEED
(JOHN CHAPMAN)
1774–1845

Probably Johnny was living in the home of one of his half-sisters near Mansfield in 1812, when the Indians decided to attack the settlers there. Certainly we know that it was Johnny who volunteered to go to the fort at Mount Vernon, Ohio, to get help from the soldiers there. On the way he warned many settlers of the impending attack.

Johnny may have been regarded as a little saint on the frontier, but it is doubtful that he took himself too seriously. When a visiting preacher chided the congregation in church one Sunday because they couldn't produce a man "who, like the primitive Christian, walks toward heaven barefoot and clad in sackcloth," Johnny was delighted to trot to the pulpit in his bare feet, wearing a shirt made out of an old coffee sack. "Here's a primitive Christian!" he shouted, and he chuckled as happily as anyone when the preacher retreated in confusion.

Johnny was in his seventy-second year when he died of pneumonia near Fort Wayne, Indiana. The orchards that Johnny planted have long since vanished, for even a tree doesn't live forever. The story of Johnny's wonderful mission hasn't vanished, however, and probably it never will. He was a unique person who lived in a marvelous time, and we will remember him and tell his story as long as there are apple trees.

Other Titles in the ValueTale Series